ARKEVIOUS ARMSTRONG

CONFII
Fro

WITHIN

60 Day Challenge

Confidence From Within: A 60 Day Challenge

Published by:
Relentless Publishing House, LLC
www.relentlesspublishing.com

Photography by: Curtis Reynolds

First Edition: February 2020

ISBN: 9781948829953

Acknowledgement

First and foremost, giving honor to the Most High. I wouldn't be where I am today if it wasn't for God's grace and mercy. My beautiful daughters, those are my "Why" because of them I push. I sacrifice so much for those girls. They give me a reason to go hard and never settle for mediocrity. To my amazing mother, thanks for being so strong and for overcoming so much including her addictions. To everyone who has supported me, believed in me, and given me words of encouragement, thank you and I really appreciate you dearly. The lives that I have changed and touched either from a video, event, my last book *Destined For Victory* or whatever our encounter was, I just want to say thank you for allowing me to be a influence in your lives.

Why is confidence so important?

Confidence is believing in yourself, feeling comfortable in your true-self, knowing that you have worth. If you are confident, people believe you. Confidence is attractive, brings success, helps to connect well with others and you generally feel happier. Only you can say that you're not confident. Others may see it. Here are some tips. How to gain confidence & maintain it:

Have positive mindset.

Learn to like, respect & love yourself.

Be social.

Go outside of your comfort zone.

Remain goal orientated & be proud of your achievements.

Accept compliments.

Do things your good at & try new things.

Accept that you & others are not perfect, you make mistakes, but accept responsibility.

Accept who you are.

Don't put things off.

Have gratitude.

Be a humble individual.

Look forward to life & the future, set goals and stick to them.

Look for solutions & ways to achieve success.

Encourage people around you & respect their views.

Respect your own views & assertively stand up for yourself.

Challenge Day 1

You can't buy the formula to success, you have to discover it on your own. Gravitate towards what makes you happy and gives you joy when you're doing what you love. Make sure your joy isn't someone else's happiness.

Suggestion

JUST DO YOU. People will always give you advice on how to live your life. There's nothing wrong with taking advice from others. As long as you are creating your own path and moving at your own pace, you will be more appreciative of your accomplishments.

Challenge Day 2

Live your life for you and not them. Your life will be so at peace when you find your peace. I can guarantee you that your happiness or joy will never rest in the hands or the opinions of someone else. Just Do You and be happy doing so.

Suggestion

Live with the consequences of your own decisions and no one else's. The key to happiness is living freely for you because we are not bound by other people's opinions of us. We can be imprisoned by our own unhappiness. However, following your own path is extremely empowering. You will look around and realize "I did this. I should be proud of myself."

Challenge Day 3

Nothing is more gratifying than knowing why you're doing something that is meaningfully serving a purpose. Wake up everyday excited about life but especially excited about your purpose. One of the most important aspects of finding your own route is the feeling you get when you realize you've done something great.

Suggestion

Take time to do for others. Doing something for yourself is one thing, but doing things for others is life-changing. Life isn't about what you can get from others, but how can you be an influence in the lives of others. Living your life with a purpose gives you a new reason for existence.

Challenge Day 4

Whatever you do, do it effectively. Do it with meaning. Make sure that the reason behind it has a purpose that will influence and push you beyond your comprehension. "WHAT'S YOUR WHY?"

Suggestion

Understand your "why" and start living your life with a purpose. Nothing is more rewarding than when you start understanding your existence in life. Execute effectively by utilizing every second and minute of your time. You are given the same 24 hours as everyone else. What you do with your 24 hours is entirely up to you. Make it count.

Challenge Day 5

How often do you stop yourself from doing something? Or wait for something else to change before you move forward? Many people are unprepared for the unexpected. They are in a rush when creating or developing something then fail to properly plan.

Suggestion

In order to plan properly you must first know what you want. Once you know what you want, do some research. Researching a path will help guide you where you are trying to go. Gather as much information about your goal. Lastly, remember a goal without an plan is just a wish. There are millions of wishful individuals in this world. You shouldn't be one of them.

Challenge Day 6

Many individuals are in a rush for something greater; either financially or a healthier lifestyle. Some will not properly think it through. Jumping into things prematurely is asking for failure. Understand this, it's not going to happen right away. Taking baby steps is an accomplishment. In order for anything to happen, I need for you to make a decision RIGHT NOW!

Suggestion

Don't rush the results. To often we get in a rush of wanting to do things right away. A goal without a plan is a plan preparing to fail. For instance, if you are interested in losing weight the first thing you must do is learn your body type. Learn the type of diet that fits your body type, know your iron level, and know your calorie intake. These are the type of things you must understand because they are pertinent to a successful outcome.

Challenge Day 7

It's important to know when you need to shift your focus. Often we find ourselves putting too much energy into other things that are not helping us reach our goals. It's not a secret. You know exactly what you need to do and you also know what's distracting you.

Suggestion

Do not allow your distractions to become a ritual. It has become a norm for you to NOT do what is necessary to advance you. If you need to focus, log out of social media and turn the television off. Even if you live by watching your favorite shows. Do yourself a favor and log out for four hours either in the beginning of the day or for a period in the afternoon.

Challenge Day 8

When you find the thing that gives you joy, happiness, and peace, that's when you've found your purpose. You must harness that thing and stay focused. Be determined by committing yourself towards accomplishing tasks daily.

Suggestion

Figure out what you love doing. The one thing that brings you joy when you do it, and it will help you find your purpose. This is something that you would do for free because it doesn't feel like work. You go to sleep and wake up thinking about it and you're always ready to tap into it. Figure it out so you can do just that!

Challenge Day 9

Remove yourself from all distractions by either surrounding yourself around driven individuals, or isolating yourself from others. Put the phone down and get off of social media. Spend some time with yourself. Do some deep soul searching. When was the last time you've tried something different?

Suggestion

You must do things differently to get something you never had. The definition of insanity is repeatedly doing the same things, yet expecting different results. Nothing CHANGES until you CHANGE. Don't be afraid to think outside the box and push yourself to higher heights. You would be amazed at what you're capable of doing.

Challenge Day 10

When you change your focus, it alters your circumstances. What areas of your life could use some massive improvement and shifts? In order for anything to change, you must first be honest with yourself. TAKE ACCOUNTABILITY! TAKE OWNERSHIP!

Suggestion

Focus on what you can do to better serve your desires to succeed. Let's just be honest, you might be where you are psychologically and financially because of the choices you've made. Better choices equal sustainable results.

Kettisha Hodges

Canton, MO

Arkevious you have inspired me personally and professionally based on your spirit, enthusiasm and passion for what you are doing. The desire you have to make a change in someone's life is displayed in the work you do, the trust you build and the charisma you display. The simple fact that you are living proof of what someone can do when they are determined, motivated and encouraged to be better. I have re-evaluated where I am taking my life based on the impact you have made in my life and the words of wisdom you have shared. You remind me that I am worth much more and I don't have to settle for mediocre based on one's view and opinion. I have to make the decision to shake up my life and chase what I believe in and what I dream to be in life.

Challenge Day 11

Don't become fixated on the things that are distracting and draining you. It's so easy to focus on the problems rather than the solutions. Mentally remove yourself from all distractions and physically surround yourself around others that are doing more or better than you.

Suggestion

When deciding what you are going to do, your decision should always determine how to make the most progress towards the goals with the time and resources available. Being focused means that you have clear goals and objectives in your work, and you're dedicated to achieving them.

Challenge Day 12

Learn how to identify certain struggles when you're becoming distracted. Either you want to succeed or you love struggling. Ask yourself, "How important is this to me? What does it mean to me?" This will indicate how serious you are about it.

Suggestion

Set aside time daily, if only five minutes, to visualize this goal. The more details you can put in the better. The "WHY" behind your the goal is crucial, as it will serve as a motivator. The emotional connect is hugely important. This will motivate you to keep moving toward your goal.

Challenge Day 13

If you focus more on the positive things about yourself and not the negative, your outcomes will be a lot different. Situations are neither negative or positive. Your thinking makes it so. Understanding what you see in yourself will be what you'll become. What you speak from your mouth will become your reality.

Suggestion

Use positive language about yourself and your ability to meet challenges and achieve your goals. This is what will show up for you externally. The words you speak will become the house you live in. They hold great truth.

Challenge Day 14

You're spending too much time on your devices, in front of your computer and even watching too much television. You spend more time doing things that are contradicting to the things you need to be focusing on. You spend more time watching others excel, rather than focusing on your own personal goals.

Suggestion

The next time you sit down to focus, turn off your notifications for any social media: Twitter, Facebook, Instagram, LinkedIn, Snapchat etc. Just try it, even for a day or just a few hours. Turn off anything that distracts you or breaks your attention. Watch how much you get accomplished by starving the things that you're normally feeding into on a daily basis.

Challenge Day 15

We have all experienced anger at some point in our lives, and it can be a real problem. It starts as a harmless feeling that can potentially grow into something dangerous and hard to control.

Suggestion

Communicate your feelings without being verbally or physically aggressive. Even if someone pushes your buttons, you always have a choice in how you respond or react. You can't always control the situation you're in or how it makes you feel. However, you can control how you express your emotions.

Challenge Day 16

Anytime you allow someone to have a negative influence over the way you think, feel, or behave you given them the power over your life. It will rob you of the mental strength that you need to reach your greatest potential.

Suggestion

Carefully decide who you allow in your life. Being resentful of people who take up too much of your energy is a sign that you aren't setting clear boundaries. People get away with what you allow them to. If you give an inch, they'll take a mile. Protect your peace and happiness by all costs.

Challenge Day 17

Some people don't like you and some people won't like your choices. You don't have to let their opinions affect how you feel about yourself. Everyone is entitled to their own opinion. Just like you're entitled to live your life as you desire too.

Suggestion

Learn to take constructive criticism as a positive and not a negative. Some people see things you don't see about yourself. You can't control the opinion of others, but what you can control is how you respond and react. Feeling bad about yourself based on what someone says or how that person feels about you gives that person too much power over you.

Challenge Day 18

A grudge won't diminish the other person's life, but it will wreak havoc on your own. Holding onto anger from the past allows an individual to occupy space in your life. Holding onto something that happened in the past, robs every opportunity of what could potentially be.

Suggestion

Learn to forgive and move forward. Holding onto hurt, pain, and having resentment towards someone doesn't help. Better yet, it hurts you more that it hurts them. I'm not saying it's easy, but it is necessary. It's necessary to want happiness and prosperity rather than being resentful and bitter. MAKE A CHOICE to be free or be bound by your past.

Challenge Day 19

When someone doubts you, it can be tempting to set out to prove them wrong. Make sure your purpose is centered around your desires to succeed and not about convincing people that you're more valuable than they give you credit for. Stop explaining yourself to those that doubt you.

Suggestion

Prove to yourself that you're deserving of any opportunity. Prove people wrong while proving to yourself that you are right. Self-love, self respect, as well as your dignity means everything. You don't owe anyone an explanation or a reason.

Challenge Day 20

Why are you attached to the type of people who seem to bring out the worst in you? You're attracted to toxic people. You know, the individuals that convince you every time out of doing the things that you should be doing. These individuals may provoke you to say things you may regret or pressure you to do things you wouldn't normally do.

Suggestion

Stay true to yourself and your values. Refuse to let others have negative influence over you. Once you give people the authority and control over how you feel or think, then you have relinquished all power to them. Surround yourself with positive individuals that are goal oriented and driven to better those around them as well.

Over the years Arkevious has inspired and pushed me to move past some of my fears. The one thing I learned from him was, "There is only one thing that makes a dream impossible to achieve, the fear of failure. No great success was ever achieved without failure." This resonated with me because I was battling with moving forward due to the fear of failure or bringing disappointment. Arkevious made me realize that failure is just a part of the process. He said to be prepared for things to fail and understand that failure is just a learning experience. I was always taught not to fail and be successful. It wasn't until listening to Arkevious' messages and reading his inspirational posts that I realize that failure is a part of becoming successful. Arkevious, I want to personally thank you for your inspiring words and messages. May it continue to reach and teach others like it did me. Be blessed!

Challenge Day 21

Have you ever started something, then second guessed it? You doubted yourself in almost everything you've tried to do. You look for the opinions of others only because you don't trust your own judgment.

Suggestion

Stop entertaining the idea of having made the wrong decision. There's no power in that. Instead, know that things are working out for your good and that you are learning and growing while you build your confidence.

Challenge Day 22

You dread to get up in the morning. You've struggled to motivate yourself each day. Nothing seems to work. You've became uninterested in anything socially, not wanting to be bothered. Just one of those days...

Suggestion

Change your routine. Try doing a few things differently. Try getting up an hour early. Try exercising or meditating. Start listening to calming music and use deep breathing techniques. These things could potentially reduce your stress level and anxiety.

Challenge Day 23

Sometimes you just lose faith in your own ability to make it work or to see it through. Giving up is too easy and trying harder is too difficult. You're too prideful to ask for help. Are you going to sit there and continue to do nothing or get up and make it happen?

Suggestion

Make a decision and own it! Usually your first reaction is going to be your best reaction, because it comes from intuition rather than from ego. Also, outside opinions have not had the opportunity to interfere. When you care about what other people think of you it will continue to hold you back.

Challenge Day 24

Negative and doubtful thinking has caused you to live in a shadow. The dark-side that we all hate but we live within its comfort. Just as we have a shadow side of us, we also have a light side. That's the positive and optimistic side about ourselves we all know that we're capable to do more than we actually do.

Suggestion

Instead of focusing on what you are lacking, focus on what you do have and what you have accomplished. This way of thinking will foster a feeling of gratitude, when you invest positive energy into your outcome.

Challenge Day 25

If you're feeling like you're the only one going through something or struggling, news flash! You're not. You're just choosing to harp upon it and allowing it to keep you in a rut.

Suggestion

Never show people you're struggling. The reason people are able to deal with their self-doubt and still achieve success is they have acknowledged it and kept it moving. KEEP IT MOVING!

Challenge Day 26

If you are afraid of putting yourself out there it's because of doubt and the fear of failure. The truth is you will fail continuously if doubting yourself becomes natural. The fear of launching or putting yourself out there never entirely ceases. Everyone gets nervous.

Suggestion

Understand that fear is a sign of affirmation. Believe it or not, fear may be a sign that you're on the right track. Doubting yourself, your abilities, and your work may actually be a sign you're doing the right thing. It may require you to push yourself beyond your norm. No one is perfect and we're all human.

Challenge Day 27

Without working on yourself and improving yourself every day, it is unrealistic for you to expect any change or anything to be different. To see change, something must change.

Suggestion

Invest in yourself. It is a great act of self love and may very well be the most profitable investment you'll ever make. That is why YOU are the most important thing you can place your time and money on.

Challenge Day 28

Stop being average and excepting mediocrity. Stop becoming complacent with the hand you were dealt. Life isn't fair nor is it easy. You deserve more and I believe you want more, but you lack confidence and courage.

Suggestion

Start investing time in acquiring knowledge and then make use of the knowledge you learned. The more you learn, the more you realize that you have a lot more to learn. Knowledge is a tool. So read books, listen to podcasts and watch videos that add value to you.

Challenge Day 29

Time management is something many people struggle with. Either people don't have the time or they don't have enough time. Either way you're wasting your time somewhere or not properly executing your time.

Suggestion

Manage your time. The secret to managing your time effectively is knowing what you want to do and when you will do it. This way, you stay proactive and in "execute" mode rather than reactive in "catch up" mode. Maximize every second and opportunity.

Challenge Day 30

Do not rush! It seems like it's not happening for you fast enough. Frustration seems to be settling in way too often. Rushing will cause you to miss out on something that is meant for you to learn from.

Suggestion

Maximize your time by following these tips: make peace with a past, set priorities, and choose quality over volume. Together these three rules can create an environment in which you can thrive. First, you need to understand them individually.

Curtis A. Le Blanc
Pennslyvania

What inspires me most about Mr. Armstrong is his determination. He believes in the gift God gave him. Even though he encountered problematic trials growing up, he believes all things are possible with God (Matthew 19:26). Old ways must die and all anxieties must be cast away (1 Peter 5:7) in pursuit of your life's purpose. Instead of giving in he is giving his all and making his impact felt in the community. I believe *Destined For Victory,* could inspire others because it has purpose. This book demands the reader to take charge of their life. It speaks about the sacrifices we must make in order to reach our maximum potential. The book is very motivational. It gives you sixty days worth of content to self-reflect upon. What I like most was the presentation of the book itself. It revealed investing in yourself is golden. Arkevious Armstrong lets his faith inspire others to fight. We all go through difficult times in life. Positivity and words of encouragement makes life easier. A major factor in determining how our lives turn out is the way we choose to focus our energy.

Challenge Day 31

Your habits will determine the distance and success for your future. You must break the bad habits and inherit good ones. The old way isn't working for you. Nothing changes until something change!

Suggestion

Your outcome reflects the habits of your day-to-day life. The habits you develop from this day forward will ultimately determine how your future pans out; rich or poor, healthy or unhealthy, fulfilled or unfulfilled, and happy or unhappy. It's your choice, so please choose wisely.

Challenge Day 32

The results of your bad habits usually don't surface or show up until later in your life when you're trying to accomplish a goal, such as losing weight or studying for an exam.

Suggestion

Don't allow yourself to be comfortable in a space of familiarity. Change is good. Change shows growth. When you develop chronic bad habits, life will eventually give you consequences. Negative habits breed negative consequences. Successful habits create positive rewards.

Challenge Day 33

Look at it this way, if you want to enjoy longevity you must have healthy habits. If you have the luxury of doing something you love every single day, you'll become great at it.

Suggestion

Try these eight tips to help you execute more efficiently:

• Try meditating or meditate more regularly.
• Try to understand your core Target.
• Be humble and gracious: appreciate what you have.
• Be cognizant of your attitude
• Help others. When you help others, in return they help you.
• Work out more, exercise more and eat healthier.
• Create routines and stick with them.
• Believe in yourself. Know that you're capable of doing all things.

Challenge Day 34

Your behavior is based on routines and rituals that you have developed over a period of time. Quit doing the same thing over and over again and expecting a different result. Nothing changes, until something changes.

Suggestion

Try something different in order to produce a different result. No matter how much you hope for the opposite, if you're wanting different results you need to change your approach even when it's painful to do so. Albert Einstein said, "insanity is doing the same thing and expecting a different result". The fact is, if you keep the same approach you will keep getting the same results.

Challenge Day 35

Your habits dictate your results. Habits will either elevate you or hold you back. Change is hard but it's necessary. It is necessary for you to make the appropriate adjustments for the life you desire.

Suggestion

Gather up the fight within and you should be good to go for what you want to achieve. Change is hard; self-discipline is even harder. When things get complicated figure out another way. Don't put off tomorrow what you can do today. Tomorrow will turn into a week and week would turn into a month. Then you'll realize you're further behind than expected.

Challenge Day 36

How do you identify bad habits especially when everyone has them? Question is, do you realize that your daily habits have brought you results that lead to nowhere. Your actions are responsible for your outcome, and if your outcome isn't what you like then change something about you.

Suggestion

Become conscious of the problem. It may sound simple or redundant, but it can be one of the most difficult steps to take in the process of overcoming negative patterns. Know what exactly you're doing and then identify the triggers. It's important to address these patterns before they become increasingly difficult to fix.

Challenge Day 37

Anybody can give their opinion about you, but only your actions determine who you really are. Take a good look at yourself. If you don't like what you see, CHANGE IT!

Suggestion

Keep your mind on what's important and not what others think. The only true opinion that matters is yours. Other people's opinion have no credibility in defining what you're all about. Simple minded individuals don't understand extraordinary people.

Challenge Day 38

It's not so much the action that defines who you are, but your personal reactions to other people's opinions. Your reactions towards people or situations solidifies your discipline and self-control.

Suggestion

Collect yourself before reacting. Pause and allow your initial emotional reaction to pass. Most of us spend the majority of our lives reacting to others or circumstances around us. Premature reaction causes us to make poor decisions.

Challenge Day 39

Your actions also determine your motivation.
Whatever it is you're inspired by or motivated to do will
dictate your actions. Your actions dictate your
outcome and your outcome is based off of your
commitment.

Suggestion

Ask yourself, "What drives me to keep going every day?
To keep pushing? What is my WHY?" Normally that
"WHY" is connected to something emotional. Use that
thing to fuel you, to elevate you and to inspire you.

Challenge Day 40

There is a proverb that states, "Good things come to those who wait." It is a well known saying which holds a lot of truth, but I have come to learn that it is a flawed saying because it is incomplete.

Suggestion

Be actively engaged as you wait. Waiting alone is not enough. Good things do not come to only those who wait, but those who also actively do something about their situation while they are waiting. In other words, faith without works is dead. Get off your butt and go make it happen.

Travis Hicks Wayne
Jenks, Oklahoma

I've been following Arkevious for a long time now.
Arkevious caught my attention because of the sincere
truth that he speaks. There are many instances where I
have been inspired by watching his videos as he shares
his wisdom and experiences with whomever will tune in
to listen. Out of all his content, what has inspired me the
most was a picture that he shared on his LinkedIn
account. This picture was a collage of smaller pictures
taken throughout the years next to a bigger picture of
himself as he is today. The smaller pictures showed
Arkevious as a younger man who was not making the
best decisions for himself. Those were the years of his life
where he really struggled. The different expressions on
his face and the look in his eyes in each one of those
pictures told a slightly different story of what he was
going through at that time. However, the larger picture,
the one that shows as he is today, showed a man of pride,
humility, triumph and eagerness. What I got from

that collage of pictures was exactly what I needed to see at that time in my life when I was going through some things. It reminded me that my life is a process and no matter what my current situation is, I need to have hope and know that with time, I can get through this trial. It also made me in awe of the transformation power of God. At the exact times those pictures of Arkevious's were taken, when things weren't going so well, I bet he never would've imagined himself as he is today. When we start making decisions that honor God, the transformational power of our God is amazing to say the least.

Challenge Day 41

Do not judge your success off other people's success. One of the things that make people impatient is seeing other people getting ahead faster than them. This is especially true if they started off at the same time and with the same resources and opportunities.

Suggestion

Know what your plan is and where you are headed as an individual. This is how you develop patience. There are many ways to achieve any one thing. The trick is to stick to your own plan when others around you seem to be getting ahead much faster than you. Yes, they may be enjoying more success than you, but you know nothing about where they are ultimately headed.

Challenge Day 42

Why should your path and your direction be determined by what others are doing? Be patient with your own plans and your own dreams. At times such as these, it is easy to leave your plan and seek a "shortcut" to success.

Suggestion

Learn to be patient with yourself. You are not perfect and will make mistakes along the way. Please understand you are on the right track and headed in the right direction. Regardless of how many mistakes and setbacks you may encounter on the way, remember don't just look forward to reaching the destination. Enjoy the journey too.

Challenge Day 43

Simply focus on what works versus what doesn't work in your personal or professionally life. Many people will find the time to focus on the wrong things. It's up to you on what you decide to put your energy into good or bad.

Suggestion

Focus on what you are good at so you can potentially become great at it. The struggle that many of us face is that we become fixated on the things we cannot change. Instead of us knuckling down on the things we are good at. So the best advice for you is to change the things you can and let go of what you can't.

Challenge Day 44

Life will hit you when you least expect it. It will cause you to become mentally and physically frustrated, and drain you. It's in your best interest to take a step back to readjust yourself in order to get back focused.

Suggestion

It's best to keep busy and plow your energy and anger into something positive. Whatever hobby or gift you have, put your energy and focus into something that will keep you busy. Some people like to workout , some people like to play basketball, and some even write music. Whatever it is that you love, allow it to be your coping skill.

Challenge Day 45

If you don't consciously set goals you're not planning to succeed. Stop making it hard for yourself. The lack of seriousness and commitment stems from being unfocused on what matters most.

Suggestion

Plan how you want your week to flow. Reflect on some things. Stop and analyze what it is you desire to accomplish. Review all angles just to be sure that you're doing everything that is necessary. FOCUS MORE and EXECUTE EFFECTIVELY.

Challenge Day 46

What is the definition of a realistic goal to you? Let's sum it up. A goal is the on going pursuit of a worthy objective until you accomplish it. How hungry are you? How serious are you? How bad do you want it.

Suggestion

Commit yourself to it daily. Wake up excited and go to bed ready to wake up to do it all over again. Never stop or give up. You have to be relentless with this mission in achieving your goals.

Challenge Day 47

The structure that you create around your goals to execute your plan, revolves around your capability to tune in and become more focused. To pursue means to not give up. You got to be hungry for this opportunity.

Suggestion

Form a solid foundation that connected to what causes you to be committed. What are you emotionally connected to that pushes you every single day to never give up? Rely on it, depend on it and use it for your benefit.

Challenge Day 48

The most important thing is you must make sure that your goals are yours. Too often we see others pursue their dreams just because someone else thought or felt that they should. STOP, THINK, and REVIEW yourself right now. Is this your plan or idea or is it what someone else wants you to do?

Suggestion

Don't allow other people or society to determine your definition of success. If you do then you've subconsciously positioned yourself for failure. It's OK to get advice, but don't allow that advice to be the final decision you make. This is your future. This is your dream. No one owes this to you. You owe this to yourself.

Challenge Day 49

Be patient. Understand that things won't always go according to your plan and that's okay. Trust in the timing. Trust in the unfolding. Trust in the simple fact that you've always found your way, even when you didn't think you would.

Suggestion

Don't be passive. Don't wish for things yet never go boldly after them. Don't expect God to answer your prayers without stepping out in faith. Don't think you're entitled to anything you aren't pursuing with your mind, your heart, and your own two hands.

Challenge Day 50

You spend too much time seeking confidence.
Sometimes people wait to feel confident before they
take action. This is a mistake because we may never
feel confident until we TRY and succeed or unless we
fail and keep trying until we get it right. If you wait for
confidence to begin, we might end up waiting for a
long time. Fail now and build confidence as you go.

Suggestion

Believe in courage. Courage is the secret sauce that
allows you to act despite your fears. Courage gives you
the ability to put aside your fear of failure and take the
first steps. Courage helps you overcome the fear of
rejection. Courage allows you to attempt things that you
have not tried before, despite your fear of looking foolish.

Challenge Day 51

Never allow your problems to become bigger than your purpose. When you stay focused on your purpose and your reason, nothing seems to catch you off guard. Subconsciously you are prepared for the unknown if it ever occurs.

Suggestion

Work toward owning every part of your realities. Not just the things that need work but also your strengths and successes. Owning all your outcomes can help teach you to do better the next time. It also allows you to see your failure as a learning experience to help you know what not to do next time.

Challenge Day 52

To fully accept your reality, it's important to acknowledge any role you may have played, good or bad, in getting where you are. Ask yourself questions related to your current situation to help work toward solutions. To fully accept your reality, it is important to identify what you may have done to foster success or failure. Once you know what you're dealing with, you can work toward the best next steps.

Suggestion

Taking accountability and responsibility is a must. Just make the appropriate changes and adjustments and watch your circumstances shift. Can you visualize the alternative if you don't make any changes? What about your health? Your relationships? If you just keep on doing the same things that you've always done, what will your lifestyle be like five years from now?

Challenge Day 53

It's easy to look in the mirror and point out all your insecurities, yet hard to face your reality. Let's start acknowledging some great attributes about yourself. Make a list of your strengths, the things you are good at, the values that you hold, and the accomplishments you've achieved. Counting on your competencies helps you realize your strengths, which in turn will help you improve your attitude toward yourself.

Suggestion

Whisper to yourself, "Every day has the power to determine the quality of your life." Train your mind with these words of encouragement and become a source of courage and hope for yourself. You'll have a strength you can rely on in hard times.

Challenge Day 54

Don't shy away from challenges. Struggles are a way of life and we have to learn to confront them. You'll never guess that the most challenging things hold the greatest opportunity for success for you.

Suggestion

The first thing you have to do is to reassess the wrong decisions that you have made to deserve this misfortune so that these types of challenges won't come back to haunt you.

Challenge Day 55

Ultimately it's your choice. Remember you are responsible for every choice you make. I suggest you choose wisely. Commit yourself now to creating goals that will guarantee you your freedom and success.

Suggestion

Focus your energy on the now. Look at the path that will get you to the life you want. Are your current choices moving you closer to where you want to go? What do you need to stop doing? In what areas do you need adjustments? What should you continue to do? You know the answers. Make a choice.

Challenge Day 56

Include steps you will take to create a new reality. Break your goal into small steps that can be accomplished one at a time to build your confidence and self-worth as you go. Your new reality can begin to happen once you have a plan with specific goals.

Suggestion

BE MORE SPECIFIC! Most people lose it by not accurately defining what they want. It's one of the main reasons individuals never achieve what they're capable of. If your goal is to lose weight and live a healthier lifestyle, what does that consist of?

Challenge Day 57

One of the biggest issues many of us have when starting something is understanding the contribution and energy that it takes to put in. Too often you put energy into the wrong things and people are expecting something more in return. Only just to get back the same you've always gotten. NOTHING!

Suggestion

Keep in mind, everyone wants the easy lifestyle. Whether it's money, cars, health or being debt-free. There is no such thing as a unrealistic goal. The only thing that is unrealistic is the fear you have within. You've allowed it to talk you out of even trying or believing in yourself.

Challenge Day 58

Where you are in life is temporary. Where you end up in life is permanent. How you get from point A to point B is entirely up to you. You can't make positive progress with a negative attitude.

Suggestion

Don't let the past immobilize you. The biggest step to changing the world around you is to change the world within you. Learn from bad choices, stupid choices and lazy choices. Your past has taught you but it doesn't define who you are as a person.

Challenge Day 59

Nothing keeps us stagnant like our own fear, impatience, and frustration. Moving forward with the right choices means we must eliminate these emotions. Holding onto something that you have full control over is pointless!

Suggestion

Write in your own words the entirety of your thoughts. The good, the bad, and the ugly. Then, jot down your choices and their potential outcomes. Predict what would happen if you did one thing versus another. Circle the choice that you believe will lead to your highest good.

Challenge Day 60

When you recognize the individuals that influence you, then you can discern whether their advice is causing positive or negative effects. Ask yourself, "To whom am I listening, when instead I should be listening to myself?"

Suggestion

Follow your intuition. This helps you realize that you have the power to make the right decisions on your own. The truth is you already know exactly what you must do and what will happen, if only you follow your internal GPS. Intuition is what feels right inside, and it isn't just some gut feeling. Your instincts can save you time and heartaches.

About the Author

Arkevious specializes in helping people to transition from average to great and from fearful to fearless. How? By teaching individuals how to operate from the mindset of expectancy and not fear. He's traveled to many places speaking to people from all walks of life. From conferences, corporate offices to leadership workshops, colleges, jails and much more. He's noticed one thing: majority of everyone had one thing in common. They struggled with "Confidence". Barely having enough confidence to get them past that threshold, not having enough confidence to break beyond that glass ceiling. The book, "Confidence From Within," will significantly help those that struggle with acceptance and accountability, something that plays a major role in how every person approaches challenges & obstacles. Knowledge is not power. Applied knowledge is power. So if you apply each day to your daily activities, one can almost guarantee that you will see a shift in your results.

Made in the USA
Middletown, DE
19 March 2020